How to Create a Blog

& Make Money

by Caprica Publishing

So, you're out of work and despite best efforts a low wage job just can't pay the bills

Maybe it's time to consider a different path! Why not consider self-employment or starting your own business blogging for yourself and others?

The good news is that there are other things you can do. Often referred to as "side hustles" these methods of making extra money can be very helpful. Let's be honest and get something right out in the open. There are no free lunches or easy money (in case you luck out with lottery tickets).

Everything worth doing and worth making money from takes time and effort

Whether it's blogging or selling knick-knacks on Etsy, you CAN and WILL make money if you're willing to put forth the effort. Although we could write a book on the subject, for now we're going to discuss blogging and how you can use your skills and years of experience to help and inform others. Whether it's simple blog or a full website, if you can type a bit and have a story to share, you can build an audience.

Blogging is something that allows business owners to reach out to a wider base of individuals and sell their products and/or services. However, most business owners are too busy running their business to bother with blogging, social media, etc. Contact some business owners you know and offer to help them with blog articles and social media posts, etc.

Feeling independent?

Maybe you're a photographer, writer, skier, boater or whatever! Use your experience to help and teach others. Get a domain name for $15 per year, a small web hosting account with a simple WordPress website and start writing. If you want someone to set all of that up for you check out https://alpinewebmedia.com . They will set you up with a full web hosting account, a full WordPress website/blog and yearly maintenance for just $359.40 per year.

Note: The above special is only for this book's readers so make sure to mention that.

Blogging can be fun!

You will find it's fun to do and you can negotiate a price that works for both you and the business owner. Also, approach organizations, etc. and offer your services. Most will welcome the chance to work with someone who can assist them with their blog articles at a much lower cost than they would pay a marketing agency. Use the blogging offer to lead into social media posts and even website content management.

Tip: Join or visit a business organization such as BNI (Business Networking International) to offer your services.

The room will be filled with all types of busy business owners hungry to find someone offering affordable services to help them with blogging, etc. Make sure you don't skimp on what you charge and negotiate a rate that both you and the business owner are happy with. Chances are that you can make a comfortable income that will beat a larger agencies fee.

Make sure that you update your blog regularly

People will usually subscribe to your blog and return on a regular basis to read the latest news. Your written content should be engaging with interesting photos, etc. to inspire your readers to comment and interact with you. If you're managing your own blog, you can make money by adding Google Ads to your blog/website and adding affiliate links. Learn more and join the Strategy for Profit Facebook group at https://www.facebook.com/groups/StrategyForProfit

Reach out to others who share a common interest or circumstance. Perhaps you love ocean cruising and wanted to share experiences and pointers with another world travelers. Maybe you are a dog lover and want your blog to address pet care issues. Blog about men or women's issues, book or movie reviews, pet peeves, current events, etc.

Use your interests and passions to focus on interesting topics for a blog

You could do a travel blog of everywhere you've been. You could do a pictorial blog sharing photos of where you've been. Blending in ads that will encourage readers to visit such places such as travel agencies, hotels, car rentals etc. will enhance the value of your blog. It's very possible to earn some extra money when readers click on these ads to secure travel, lodging or a car rental, etc.

If you're creating great, unique content, visitors will eventually start to associate your blog with great, "can't miss" content. Once you've started to build a following and traffic, lead visitors from your blog to your website, where maybe you're selling goods or services online.

Integrate your individual personality into your writing. Otherwise you may risk sounding constrained and phony. Readers can often tell if you are trying to be something other than who or what you really are.

Blogging is a personal way to get to know your customers

A visitors first impression of your blog should be a great one! That is the essence of what blogging truly is. Become an authority figure. It needn't be politically, racially, or socially motivated, but either way, when you share your thoughts with the world and hit the publish button, you are becoming an authority figure.

Most importantly, don't forget to educate yourself in your chosen niche. If you blog about great travel tips for vacationers, read as much literature on the topic as you can find.

Get in touch with other bloggers and friends. Exchange links with them and offer to feature their articles on your blog. Look for fellow bloggers who have a similar audience. Always be on the lookout for new bloggers who can help you share your content and make sure you return the favor.

For more info and resources, visit http://capricapublishing.net

BLOG PLANNER

BLOG TITLE:

DOMAIN:

TARGET AUDIENCE:

NICHE OVERVIEW:

MAIN FOCUS:

PRIMARY KEYWORDS:

MAIN TRAFFIC SOURCES:

BLOG CONTROLS

ADMIN LOGIN:

AFFILIATE ACCOUNTS:　　　　　　　　**ADVERTISER ACCOUNTS:**

HOSTING ACCOUNT LOGIN:

Important Contacts

PARTNERS:　　　　　　　　　　　　　**OTHER:**

SOCIAL MEDIA

TWITTER	FACEBOOK

INSTAGRAM	PINTEREST

OTHER	OTHER

OTHER	OTHER

BRAND CREATION

SLOGAN / TAGLINE:

WRITING & CONTENT STYLE:

NICHE SUMMARY:

6 WORDS TO DESCRIBE MY BLOG:

HOW MY BLOG PROVIDES VALUE:

MISSION STATEMENT:

BLOG DESIGN

BLOG STYLE IDEAS

THEME USED:

BASE COLOR SCHEME:

PRIMARY FONTS USED:

LOGO / GRAPHIC DESIGNER:

DESIGN CHECKLIST:

- Verify responsive design
- Create 404 landing page
- Install contact form & opt in
- Create advertiser side widgets
- Test links in navigation menu
- Install Cookie Permission Plugin
- Install Privacy Agreement

PLUGIN CHECKLIST:

- Install SEO plugin
- Install WP Total Cache
- Install social sharing plugin
- Install WP Forms
- Install Google Analytics
- Install Backup Plugin
- Install Opt-in Plugin

AFFILIATE INCOME

ADVERTISER ACCOUNTS: **AFFILIATE ACCOUNTS:**

JANUARY

TASKS, MARKETING, ENGAGEMENT & MONETIZATION

CONTENT IDEAS

PROMOTION IDEAS

TOP PRIORITIES

MONTHLY FOCUS

MONETIZATION IDEAS

MONTHLY GOALS

MAIN OBJECTIVE:

GOAL:

ACTION STEPS:

GOAL:

ACTION STEPS:

GOAL:

ACTION STEPS:

TRAFFIC STATS:

MAILING LIST SUBSCRIBERS:

CONTENT PLANNER

POST TITLE:

PUBLICATION DATE:

TARGETED KEYWORDS:

TO DO CHECKLIST:

- Research Topic
- Pinpoint Target Audience
- Choose target keywords
- Optimize for search engines
- Link to other blog post
- Create post images
- Proofread & Edit Post
- Schedule Post Date

SOCIAL SHARING: (circle all that apply)

TOPIC OUTLINE:

NOTES:

CONTENT PLANNER

CATEGORY:

RESOURCE LINKS:

GRAPHICS/IMAGES:

KEY POINTS:

SEO CHECKLIST:

- [ ] Primary keyword in post title
- [ ] Secondary keyword in sub-title
- [ ] Keyword in first paragraph
- [ ] Word count > 1000 words
- [ ] 1-2 Outbound Links
- [ ] Internal Link Structure
- [ ] Post URL includes keywords
- [ ] Meta description added
- [ ] Post includes images
- [ ] Post includes sub-headlines
- [ ] Social sharing enabled

NOTES:

POST PLANNER

WEEK OF: _____

TYPE: ARTICLE: ☐   TUTORIAL: ☐   REVIEW: ☐   GUEST POST: ☐

PUBLICATION DATE:

TITLE:
CATEGORY:
KEYWORDS:
NOTES:

PUBLICATION DATE:

TITLE:
CATEGORY:
KEYWORDS:
NOTES:

PUBLICATION DATE:

TITLE:
CATEGORY:
KEYWORDS:
NOTES:

POST PLANNER

WEEK OF: _____

TYPE: ARTICLE: ☐   TUTORIAL: ☐   REVIEW: ☐   GUEST POST: ☐

PUBLICATION DATE:

TITLE:

CATEGORY:

KEYWORDS:

NOTES:

LIST BUILDING PROGRESS:

 # SUBSCRIBERS: _____   **EMAILED THIS WEEK** ✉

SOCIAL MEDIA PROMO THIS WEEK:

☐ Twitter   ☐ Facebook   ☐ Pinterest   ☐ Instagram   ☐ YouTube   ☐ LinkedIn   ☐ Google+

EXTERNAL LINKS:

PRODUCTS PROMOTED:

INTERNAL LINKS:

☐ Affiliate Disclaimer Included

MARKETING PLANNER

TOP TRAFFIC CHANNELS:

MARKETING TO DO LIST:

FREE ADVERTISING IDEAS:

PAID ADVERTISING IDEAS:

MARKETING PLANNER

PROMOTIONAL STRATEGIES TO MAXIMIZE EXPOSURE

PROMOTIONAL IDEAS:

MARKETING TO DO:

SOCIAL MEDIA GROWTH TRACKER:

BEFORE: AFTER:

- Facebook
- Instagram
- Twitter
- Pinterest
- YouTube

OTHER:

LIST BUILDING & ENGAGEMENT:

MAILING LIST SUBSCRIBERS:

OF EMAILS SENT TO SUBSCRIBERS:

OF NEW BLOG POSTS THIS WEEK:

OF COMPLETED GUEST POSTS:

NOTES:

GUEST BLOGGING

POST TITLE:

PUBLISH DATE: | CATEGORY:

MAIN TOPIC:

POST SUMMARY:

KEY POINTS:

INCLUDED LINKS: | SHARED ON: | FACEBOOK | INSTAGRAM
| | TWITTER | PINTEREST

TAGS & KEYWORDS:

OF COMMENTS: | # OF TRACKBACKS:

NOTES:

FEBRUARY

TASKS, MARKETING, ENGAGEMENT & MONETIZATION

CONTENT IDEAS

PROMOTION IDEAS

TOP PRIORITIES

MONTHLY FOCUS

MONETIZATION IDEAS

MONTHLY GOALS

MAIN OBJECTIVE:

GOAL:

ACTION STEPS:

GOAL:

ACTION STEPS:

GOAL:

ACTION STEPS:

TRAFFIC STATS:

MAILING LIST SUBSCRIBERS:

CONTENT PLANNER

POST TITLE:

PUBLICATION DATE:

TARGETED KEYWORDS:

TO DO CHECKLIST:

- Research Topic
- Pinpoint Target Audience
- Choose target keywords
- Optimize for search engines
- Link to other blog post
- Create post images
- Proofread & Edit Post
- Schedule Post Date

SOCIAL SHARING: (circle all that apply)

Facebook Twitter YouTube Pinterest LinkedIn Instagram

TOPIC OUTLINE:

NOTES:

CONTENT PLANNER

CATEGORY:

RESOURCE LINKS:

GRAPHICS/IMAGES:

KEY POINTS:

SEO CHECKLIST:

- Primary keyword in post title
- Secondary keyword in sub-title
- Keyword in first paragraph
- Word count > 1000 words
- 1-2 Outbound Links
- Internal Link Structure
- Post URL includes keywords
- Meta description added
- Post includes images
- Post includes sub-headlines
- Social sharing enabled

NOTES:

POST PLANNER

WEEK OF: _____

TYPE: ARTICLE: TUTORIAL: REVIEW: GUEST POST:

PUBLICATION DATE:

TITLE:

CATEGORY:

KEYWORDS:

NOTES:

PUBLICATION DATE:

TITLE:

CATEGORY:

KEYWORDS:

NOTES:

PUBLICATION DATE:

TITLE:

CATEGORY:

KEYWORDS:

NOTES:

POST PLANNER

WEEK OF: _____

TYPE: ARTICLE: ☐ TUTORIAL: ☐ REVIEW: ☐ GUEST POST: ☐

PUBLICATION DATE:

TITLE:
CATEGORY:
KEYWORDS:
NOTES:

LIST BUILDING PROGRESS:

 # SUBSCRIBERS: _____ **EMAILED THIS WEEK** ✉

SOCIAL MEDIA PROMO THIS WEEK:

☐ Twitter ☐ Facebook ☐ Pinterest ☐ Instagram ☐ YouTube ☐ LinkedIn ☐ Google+

EXTERNAL LINKS:

INTERNAL LINKS:

PRODUCTS PROMOTED:

Affiliate Disclaimer Included

POST PLANNER

WEEK OF: _____

TYPE: ARTICLE: ☐   TUTORIAL: ☐   REVIEW: ☐   GUEST POST: ☐

PUBLICATION DATE:

TITLE:
CATEGORY:
KEYWORDS:
NOTES:

LIST BUILDING PROGRESS:

 # SUBSCRIBERS: _____   ☐ **EMAILED THIS WEEK** ✉

SOCIAL MEDIA PROMO THIS WEEK:

☐ Twitter   ☐ Facebook   ☐ Pinterest   ☐ Instagram   ☐ YouTube   ☐ LinkedIn   ☐ Google+

EXTERNAL LINKS:

INTERNAL LINKS:

PRODUCTS PROMOTED:

☐ Affiliate Disclaimer Included

MARKETING PLANNER

TOP TRAFFIC CHANNELS:

MARKETING TO DO LIST:

FREE ADVERTISING IDEAS:

PAID ADVERTISING IDEAS:

MARKETING PLANNER

PROMOTIONAL STRATEGIES TO MAXIMIZE EXPOSURE

PROMOTIONAL IDEAS:

MARKETING TO DO:

SOCIAL MEDIA GROWTH TRACKER:

	BEFORE:	AFTER:
Facebook		
Instagram		
Twitter		
Pinterest		
YouTube		

OTHER:

LIST BUILDING & ENGAGEMENT:

MAILING LIST SUBSCRIBERS:

 # OF EMAILS SENT TO SUBSCRIBERS:

 # OF NEW BLOG POSTS THIS WEEK:

 # OF COMPLETED GUEST POSTS:

NOTES:

GUEST BLOGGING

POST TITLE:

PUBLISH DATE:

CATEGORY:

MAIN TOPIC:

POST SUMMARY:

KEY POINTS:

INCLUDED LINKS:

SHARED ON:
- FACEBOOK
- INSTAGRAM
- TWITTER
- PINTEREST

TAGS & KEYWORDS:

OF COMMENTS:

OF TRACKBACKS:

NOTES:

MARCH

TASKS, MARKETING, ENGAGEMENT & MONETIZATION

CONTENT IDEAS

PROMOTION IDEAS

TOP PRIORITIES

MONTHLY FOCUS

MONETIZATION IDEAS

MONTHLY GOALS

MAIN OBJECTIVE:

GOAL:

ACTION STEPS:

GOAL:

ACTION STEPS:

GOAL:

ACTION STEPS:

TRAFFIC STATS:

MAILING LIST SUBSCRIBERS:

CONTENT PLANNER

POST TITLE:

PUBLICATION DATE:

TARGETED KEYWORDS:

TO DO CHECKLIST:

- Research Topic
- Pinpoint Target Audience
- Choose target keywords
- Optimize for search engines
- Link to other blog post
- Create post images
- Proofread & Edit Post
- Schedule Post Date

SOCIAL SHARING: (circle all that apply)

Facebook Twitter YouTube Pinterest LinkedIn Instagram

TOPIC OUTLINE:

NOTES:

CONTENT PLANNER

CATEGORY:

RESOURCE LINKS:

GRAPHICS/IMAGES:

KEY POINTS:

SEO CHECKLIST:

- Primary keyword in post title
- Secondary keyword in sub-title
- Keyword in first paragraph
- Word count > 1000 words
- 1-2 Outbound Links
- Internal Link Structure
- Post URL includes keywords
- Meta description added
- Post includes images
- Post includes sub-headlines
- Social sharing enabled

NOTES:

POST PLANNER

WEEK OF: _____

TYPE: ARTICLE: ☐   TUTORIAL: ☐   REVIEW: ☐   GUEST POST: ☐

PUBLICATION DATE:

TITLE: _____
CATEGORY: _____
KEYWORDS: _____
NOTES: _____

PUBLICATION DATE:

TITLE: _____
CATEGORY: _____
KEYWORDS: _____
NOTES: _____

PUBLICATION DATE:

TITLE: _____
CATEGORY: _____
KEYWORDS: _____
NOTES: _____

POST PLANNER

WEEK OF: _____

TYPE: ARTICLE: ☐   TUTORIAL: ☐   REVIEW: ☐   GUEST POST: ☐

PUBLICATION DATE:

TITLE:	
CATEGORY:	
KEYWORDS:	
NOTES:	

LIST BUILDING PROGRESS:

 # SUBSCRIBERS: _____   ☐ EMAILED THIS WEEK ✉

SOCIAL MEDIA PROMO THIS WEEK:

☐ Twitter   ☐ Facebook   ☐ Pinterest   ☐ Instagram   ☐ YouTube   ☐ LinkedIn   ☐ Google+

EXTERNAL LINKS:

PRODUCTS PROMOTED:

INTERNAL LINKS:

☐ Affiliate Disclaimer Included

POST PLANNER

WEEK OF: _____

TYPE: ARTICLE: ☐   TUTORIAL: ☐   REVIEW: ☐   GUEST POST: ☐

PUBLICATION DATE:

TITLE:

CATEGORY:

KEYWORDS:

NOTES:

LIST BUILDING PROGRESS:

 # SUBSCRIBERS: _____ ☐ **EMAILED THIS WEEK** ✉

SOCIAL MEDIA PROMO THIS WEEK:

☐ Twitter   ☐ Facebook   ☐ Pinterest   ☐ Instagram   ☐ YouTube   ☐ LinkedIn   ☐ Google+

EXTERNAL LINKS:

PRODUCTS PROMOTED:

INTERNAL LINKS:

☐ Affiliate Disclaimer Included

MARKETING PLANNER

TOP TRAFFIC CHANNELS:

MARKETING TO DO LIST:

FREE ADVERTISING IDEAS:

PAID ADVERTISING IDEAS:

MARKETING PLANNER

PROMOTIONAL STRATEGIES TO MAXIMIZE EXPOSURE

PROMOTIONAL IDEAS:

MARKETING TO DO:

SOCIAL MEDIA GROWTH TRACKER:

	BEFORE:	AFTER:
Facebook		
Instagram		
Twitter		
Pinterest		
YouTube		
OTHER:		

LIST BUILDING & ENGAGEMENT:

MAILING LIST SUBSCRIBERS:	
# OF EMAILS SENT TO SUBSCRIBERS:	
# OF NEW BLOG POSTS THIS WEEK:	
# OF COMPLETED GUEST POSTS:	

NOTES:

GUEST BLOGGING

POST TITLE:

PUBLISH DATE:	CATEGORY:

MAIN TOPIC:

POST SUMMARY:

KEY POINTS:

INCLUDED LINKS:

SHARED ON:

FACEBOOK	INSTAGRAM
TWITTER	PINTEREST

TAGS & KEYWORDS:

OF COMMENTS: # OF TRACKBACKS:

NOTES:

APRIL

TASKS, MARKETING, ENGAGEMENT & MONETIZATION

CONTENT IDEAS

PROMOTION IDEAS

TOP PRIORITIES

MONTHLY FOCUS

MONETIZATION IDEAS

MONTHLY GOALS

MAIN OBJECTIVE:

GOAL:

ACTION STEPS:

GOAL:

ACTION STEPS:

GOAL:

ACTION STEPS:

TRAFFIC STATS:

MAILING LIST SUBSCRIBERS:

CONTENT PLANNER

POST TITLE:

PUBLICATION DATE:

TARGETED KEYWORDS:

TO DO CHECKLIST:

- Research Topic
- Pinpoint Target Audience
- Choose target keywords
- Optimize for search engines
- Link to other blog post
- Create post images
- Proofread & Edit Post
- Schedule Post Date

SOCIAL SHARING: (circle all that apply)

Facebook Twitter YouTube Pinterest LinkedIn Instagram

TOPIC OUTLINE:

NOTES:

CONTENT PLANNER

CATEGORY:

RESOURCE LINKS:

GRAPHICS/IMAGES:

KEY POINTS:

SEO CHECKLIST:

- Primary keyword in post title
- Secondary keyword in sub-title
- Keyword in first paragraph
- Word count > 1000 words
- 1-2 Outbound Links
- Internal Link Structure
- Post URL includes keywords
- Meta description added
- Post includes images
- Post includes sub-headlines
- Social sharing enabled

NOTES:

POST PLANNER

WEEK OF: _____

TYPE: ARTICLE: ☐   TUTORIAL: ☐   REVIEW: ☐   GUEST POST: ☐

PUBLICATION DATE:

TITLE:

CATEGORY:

KEYWORDS:

NOTES:

PUBLICATION DATE:

TITLE:

CATEGORY:

KEYWORDS:

NOTES:

PUBLICATION DATE:

TITLE:

CATEGORY:

KEYWORDS:

NOTES:

POST PLANNER

WEEK OF: _____

TYPE: ARTICLE: ☐   TUTORIAL: ☐   REVIEW: ☐   GUEST POST: ☐

PUBLICATION DATE:

TITLE: _____
CATEGORY: _____
KEYWORDS: _____
NOTES: _____
_____

LIST BUILDING PROGRESS:

 # SUBSCRIBERS: _____ ☐ **EMAILED THIS WEEK** ✉

SOCIAL MEDIA PROMO THIS WEEK:

☐ Twitter   ☐ Facebook   ☐ Pinterest   ☐ Instagram   ☐ YouTube   ☐ LinkedIn   ☐ Google+

EXTERNAL LINKS:

INTERNAL LINKS:

PRODUCTS PROMOTED:

Affiliate Disclaimer Included

POST PLANNER

WEEK OF: _____

TYPE: ARTICLE: ☐   TUTORIAL: ☐   REVIEW: ☐   GUEST POST: ☐

PUBLICATION DATE:

TITLE:
CATEGORY:
KEYWORDS:
NOTES:

LIST BUILDING PROGRESS:

 # SUBSCRIBERS: _____   ☐ **EMAILED THIS WEEK** ✉

SOCIAL MEDIA PROMO THIS WEEK:

☐ Twitter   ☐ Facebook   ☐ Pinterest   ☐ Instagram   ☐ YouTube   ☐ LinkedIn   ☐ Google+

EXTERNAL LINKS:

INTERNAL LINKS:

PRODUCTS PROMOTED:

☐ Affiliate Disclaimer Included

MARKETING PLANNER

TOP TRAFFIC CHANNELS:

MARKETING TO DO LIST:

FREE ADVERTISING IDEAS:

PAID ADVERTISING IDEAS:

MARKETING PLANNER

PROMOTIONAL STRATEGIES TO MAXIMIZE EXPOSURE

PROMOTIONAL IDEAS:

MARKETING TO DO:

SOCIAL MEDIA GROWTH TRACKER:

BEFORE: AFTER:

- Facebook
- Instagram
- Twitter
- Pinterest
- YouTube

OTHER:

LIST BUILDING & ENGAGEMENT:

MAILING LIST SUBSCRIBERS:

OF EMAILS SENT TO SUBSCRIBERS:

OF NEW BLOG POSTS THIS WEEK:

OF COMPLETED GUEST POSTS:

NOTES:

GUEST BLOGGING

POST TITLE:

PUBLISH DATE:	CATEGORY:

MAIN TOPIC:

POST SUMMARY:

KEY POINTS:

INCLUDED LINKS:

SHARED ON:

FACEBOOK　　INSTAGRAM

TWITTER　　PINTEREST

TAGS & KEYWORDS:

OF COMMENTS:　　# OF TRACKBACKS:

NOTES:

MAY

TASKS, MARKETING, ENGAGEMENT & MONETIZATION

CONTENT IDEAS

PROMOTION IDEAS

TOP PRIORITIES

MONTHLY FOCUS

MONETIZATION IDEAS

MONTHLY GOALS

MAIN OBJECTIVE:

GOAL:

ACTION STEPS:

GOAL:

ACTION STEPS:

GOAL:

ACTION STEPS:

TRAFFIC STATS:

MAILING LIST SUBSCRIBERS:

CONTENT PLANNER

POST TITLE:

PUBLICATION DATE:

TARGETED KEYWORDS:

TO DO CHECKLIST:

- Research Topic
- Pinpoint Target Audience
- Choose target keywords
- Optimize for search engines
- Link to other blog post
- Create post images
- Proofread & Edit Post
- Schedule Post Date

SOCIAL SHARING: (circle all that apply)

Facebook Twitter YouTube Pinterest LinkedIn Instagram

TOPIC OUTLINE:

NOTES:

CONTENT PLANNER

CATEGORY:

RESOURCE LINKS:

GRAPHICS/IMAGES:

KEY POINTS:

SEO CHECKLIST:

- Primary keyword in post title
- Secondary keyword in sub-title
- Keyword in first paragraph
- Word count > 1000 words
- 1-2 Outbound Links
- Internal Link Structure
- Post URL includes keywords
- Meta description added
- Post includes images
- Post includes sub-headlines
- Social sharing enabled

NOTES:

POST PLANNER

WEEK OF: _____

TYPE: ARTICLE: ☐   TUTORIAL: ☐   REVIEW: ☐   GUEST POST: ☐

PUBLICATION DATE:

TITLE:
CATEGORY:
KEYWORDS:
NOTES:

PUBLICATION DATE:

TITLE:
CATEGORY:
KEYWORDS:
NOTES:

PUBLICATION DATE:

TITLE:
CATEGORY:
KEYWORDS:
NOTES:

POST PLANNER

WEEK OF: _____

TYPE: ARTICLE: ☐   TUTORIAL: ☐   REVIEW: ☐   GUEST POST: ☐

PUBLICATION DATE:

TITLE: _____

CATEGORY: _____

KEYWORDS: _____

NOTES: _____

LIST BUILDING PROGRESS:

 # SUBSCRIBERS: _____   **EMAILED THIS WEEK** ✉

SOCIAL MEDIA PROMO THIS WEEK:

☐ Twitter   ☐ Facebook   ☐ Pinterest   ☐ Instagram   ☐ YouTube   ☐ LinkedIn   ☐ Google+

EXTERNAL LINKS:

PRODUCTS PROMOTED:

INTERNAL LINKS:

Affiliate Disclaimer Included

POST PLANNER

WEEK OF: _____

TYPE: ARTICLE: TUTORIAL: REVIEW: GUEST POST:

PUBLICATION DATE:

TITLE:

CATEGORY:

KEYWORDS:

NOTES:

LIST BUILDING PROGRESS:

 # SUBSCRIBERS: _____   **EMAILED THIS WEEK** ✉

SOCIAL MEDIA PROMO THIS WEEK:

🐦   f   📌   📷   ▶   in   g+

EXTERNAL LINKS:

PRODUCTS PROMOTED:

INTERNAL LINKS:

Affiliate Disclaimer Included

MARKETING PLANNER

TOP TRAFFIC CHANNELS:

MARKETING TO DO LIST:

FREE ADVERTISING IDEAS:

PAID ADVERTISING IDEAS:

MARKETING PLANNER

PROMOTIONAL STRATEGIES TO MAXIMIZE EXPOSURE

PROMOTIONAL IDEAS:

MARKETING TO DO:

SOCIAL MEDIA GROWTH TRACKER:

BEFORE: AFTER:

- f
- Instagram
- Twitter
- Pinterest
- YouTube

OTHER:

LIST BUILDING & ENGAGEMENT:

MAILING LIST SUBSCRIBERS:

OF EMAILS SENT TO SUBSCRIBERS:

OF NEW BLOG POSTS THIS WEEK:

OF COMPLETED GUEST POSTS:

NOTES:

GUEST BLOGGING

POST TITLE:

PUBLISH DATE: | CATEGORY:

MAIN TOPIC:

POST SUMMARY:

KEY POINTS:

INCLUDED LINKS: | **SHARED ON:** | FACEBOOK | INSTAGRAM
| | TWITTER | PINTEREST

TAGS & KEYWORDS: | # OF COMMENTS: | # OF TRACKBACKS:

NOTES:

JUNE

TASKS, MARKETING, ENGAGEMENT & MONETIZATION

CONTENT IDEAS

PROMOTION IDEAS

TOP PRIORITIES

MONTHLY FOCUS

MONETIZATION IDEAS

MONTHLY GOALS

MAIN OBJECTIVE:

GOAL:

ACTION STEPS:

GOAL:

ACTION STEPS:

GOAL:

ACTION STEPS:

TRAFFIC STATS:

MAILING LIST SUBSCRIBERS:

CONTENT PLANNER

POST TITLE:

PUBLICATION DATE:

TARGETED KEYWORDS:

TO DO CHECKLIST:

- Research Topic
- Pinpoint Target Audience
- Choose target keywords
- Optimize for search engines
- Link to other blog post
- Create post images
- Proofread & Edit Post
- Schedule Post Date

SOCIAL SHARING: (circle all that apply)

Facebook Twitter YouTube Pinterest LinkedIn Instagram

TOPIC OUTLINE:

NOTES:

CONTENT PLANNER

CATEGORY:

RESOURCE LINKS:

GRAPHICS/IMAGES:

KEY POINTS:

SEO CHECKLIST:

- Primary keyword in post title
- Secondary keyword in sub-title
- Keyword in first paragraph
- Word count > 1000 words
- 1-2 Outbound Links
- Internal Link Structure
- Post URL includes keywords
- Meta description added
- Post includes images
- Post includes sub-headlines
- Social sharing enabled

NOTES:

POST PLANNER

WEEK OF: _____

TYPE: ARTICLE: TUTORIAL: REVIEW: GUEST POST:

PUBLICATION DATE:

TITLE:

CATEGORY:

KEYWORDS:

NOTES:

PUBLICATION DATE:

TITLE:

CATEGORY:

KEYWORDS:

NOTES:

PUBLICATION DATE:

TITLE:

CATEGORY:

KEYWORDS:

NOTES:

POST PLANNER

WEEK OF: _____

TYPE: ARTICLE: ☐ TUTORIAL: ☐ REVIEW: ☐ GUEST POST: ☐

PUBLICATION DATE:

TITLE:

CATEGORY:

KEYWORDS:

NOTES:

LIST BUILDING PROGRESS:

 # SUBSCRIBERS: _____ **EMAILED THIS WEEK** ✉

SOCIAL MEDIA PROMO THIS WEEK:

☐ Twitter ☐ Facebook ☐ Pinterest ☐ Instagram ☐ YouTube ☐ LinkedIn ☐ Google+

EXTERNAL LINKS:

INTERNAL LINKS:

PRODUCTS PROMOTED:

☐ Affiliate Disclaimer Included

POST PLANNER

WEEK OF: _____

TYPE: ARTICLE: ☐   TUTORIAL: ☐   REVIEW: ☐   GUEST POST: ☐

PUBLICATION DATE:

TITLE:
CATEGORY:
KEYWORDS:
NOTES:

LIST BUILDING PROGRESS:

 # SUBSCRIBERS: _____   ☐ **EMAILED THIS WEEK** ✉

SOCIAL MEDIA PROMO THIS WEEK:

☐ Twitter   ☐ Facebook   ☐ Pinterest   ☐ Instagram   ☐ YouTube   ☐ LinkedIn   ☐ Google+

EXTERNAL LINKS:

INTERNAL LINKS:

PRODUCTS PROMOTED:

☐ Affiliate Disclaimer Included

MARKETING PLANNER

TOP TRAFFIC CHANNELS:

MARKETING TO DO LIST:

FREE ADVERTISING IDEAS:

PAID ADVERTISING IDEAS:

MARKETING PLANNER

PROMOTIONAL STRATEGIES TO MAXIMIZE EXPOSURE

PROMOTIONAL IDEAS:

MARKETING TO DO:

SOCIAL MEDIA GROWTH TRACKER:

	BEFORE:	AFTER:
facebook		
instagram		
twitter		
pinterest		
youtube		
OTHER:		

LIST BUILDING & ENGAGEMENT:

MAILING LIST SUBSCRIBERS:	
# OF EMAILS SENT TO SUBSCRIBERS:	
# OF NEW BLOG POSTS THIS WEEK:	
# OF COMPLETED GUEST POSTS:	

NOTES:

GUEST BLOGGING

POST TITLE:

PUBLISH DATE: CATEGORY:

MAIN TOPIC:

POST SUMMARY:

KEY POINTS:

INCLUDED LINKS: SHARED ON: FACEBOOK   INSTAGRAM

                                       TWITTER   PINTEREST

TAGS & KEYWORDS: # OF COMMENTS: # OF TRACKBACKS:

                              NOTES:

JULY

TASKS, MARKETING, ENGAGEMENT & MONETIZATION

CONTENT IDEAS	PROMOTION IDEAS

TOP PRIORITIES

MONTHLY FOCUS	MONETIZATION IDEAS

MONTHLY GOALS

MAIN OBJECTIVE:

GOAL:

ACTION STEPS:

GOAL:

ACTION STEPS:

GOAL:

ACTION STEPS:

TRAFFIC STATS:

MAILING LIST SUBSCRIBERS:

CONTENT PLANNER

POST TITLE:

PUBLICATION DATE:

TARGETED KEYWORDS:

TO DO CHECKLIST:

- Research Topic
- Pinpoint Target Audience
- Choose target keywords
- Optimize for search engines
- Link to other blog post
- Create post images
- Proofread & Edit Post
- Schedule Post Date

SOCIAL SHARING: (circle all that apply)

Facebook   Twitter   YouTube   Pinterest   LinkedIn   Instagram

TOPIC OUTLINE:

NOTES:

CONTENT PLANNER

CATEGORY:

RESOURCE LINKS:

GRAPHICS/IMAGES:

KEY POINTS:

SEO CHECKLIST:

- Primary keyword in post title
- Secondary keyword in sub-title
- Keyword in first paragraph
- Word count > 1000 words
- 1-2 Outbound Links
- Internal Link Structure
- Post URL includes keywords
- Meta description added
- Post includes images
- Post includes sub-headlines
- Social sharing enabled

NOTES:

POST PLANNER

WEEK OF: _____

TYPE: ARTICLE: ☐   TUTORIAL: ☐   REVIEW: ☐   GUEST POST: ☐

PUBLICATION DATE:

TITLE:

CATEGORY:

KEYWORDS:

NOTES:

PUBLICATION DATE:

TITLE:

CATEGORY:

KEYWORDS:

NOTES:

PUBLICATION DATE:

TITLE:

CATEGORY:

KEYWORDS:

NOTES:

POST PLANNER

WEEK OF: _____

TYPE: ARTICLE: ☐   TUTORIAL: ☐   REVIEW: ☐   GUEST POST: ☐

PUBLICATION DATE:

TITLE: _____

CATEGORY: _____

KEYWORDS: _____

NOTES: _____

LIST BUILDING PROGRESS:

 # SUBSCRIBERS: _____   ☐ **EMAILED THIS WEEK** ✉

SOCIAL MEDIA PROMO THIS WEEK:

☐ Twitter   ☐ Facebook   ☐ Pinterest   ☐ Instagram   ☐ YouTube   ☐ LinkedIn   ☐ Google+

EXTERNAL LINKS:

PRODUCTS PROMOTED:

INTERNAL LINKS:

☐ Affiliate Disclaimer Included

MARKETING PLANNER

TOP TRAFFIC CHANNELS:

MARKETING TO DO LIST:

FREE ADVERTISING IDEAS:

PAID ADVERTISING IDEAS:

MARKETING PLANNER

PROMOTIONAL STRATEGIES TO MAXIMIZE EXPOSURE

PROMOTIONAL IDEAS:

MARKETING TO DO:

SOCIAL MEDIA GROWTH TRACKER:

BEFORE: AFTER:

- Facebook
- Instagram
- Twitter
- Pinterest
- YouTube

OTHER:

LIST BUILDING & ENGAGEMENT:

MAILING LIST SUBSCRIBERS:

OF EMAILS SENT TO SUBSCRIBERS:

OF NEW BLOG POSTS THIS WEEK:

OF COMPLETED GUEST POSTS:

NOTES:

GUEST BLOGGING

POST TITLE:

| PUBLISH DATE: | CATEGORY: |

MAIN TOPIC:

POST SUMMARY:

KEY POINTS:

INCLUDED LINKS:

SHARED ON:

FACEBOOK   INSTAGRAM

TWITTER   PINTEREST

TAGS & KEYWORDS:

 # OF COMMENTS: **# OF TRACKBACKS:**

NOTES:

AUGUST

TASKS, MARKETING, ENGAGEMENT & MONETIZATION

CONTENT IDEAS

PROMOTION IDEAS

TOP PRIORITIES

MONTHLY FOCUS

MONETIZATION IDEAS

MONTHLY GOALS

MAIN OBJECTIVE:

GOAL:

ACTION STEPS:

GOAL:

ACTION STEPS:

GOAL:

ACTION STEPS:

TRAFFIC STATS:

MAILING LIST SUBSCRIBERS:

CONTENT PLANNER

POST TITLE:

TARGETED KEYWORDS:

PUBLICATION DATE:

TO DO CHECKLIST:

- Research Topic
- Pinpoint Target Audience
- Choose target keywords
- Optimize for search engines
- Link to other blog post
- Create post images
- Proofread & Edit Post
- Schedule Post Date

SOCIAL SHARING: (circle all that apply)

Facebook Twitter YouTube Pinterest LinkedIn Instagram

TOPIC OUTLINE:

NOTES:

CONTENT PLANNER

CATEGORY:

RESOURCE LINKS:

GRAPHICS/IMAGES:

KEY POINTS:

SEO CHECKLIST:

- Primary keyword in post title
- Secondary keyword in sub-title
- Keyword in first paragraph
- Word count > 1000 words
- 1-2 Outbound Links
- Internal Link Structure
- Post URL includes keywords
- Meta description added
- Post includes images
- Post includes sub-headlines
- Social sharing enabled

NOTES:

POST PLANNER

WEEK OF: _____

TYPE: ARTICLE: ☐   TUTORIAL: ☐   REVIEW: ☐   GUEST POST: ☐

PUBLICATION DATE:

TITLE:
CATEGORY:
KEYWORDS:
NOTES:

PUBLICATION DATE:

TITLE:
CATEGORY:
KEYWORDS:
NOTES:

PUBLICATION DATE:

TITLE:
CATEGORY:
KEYWORDS:
NOTES:

POST PLANNER

WEEK OF: _____

TYPE: ARTICLE: ☐   TUTORIAL: ☐   REVIEW: ☐   GUEST POST: ☐

PUBLICATION DATE:

TITLE:

CATEGORY:

KEYWORDS:

NOTES:

LIST BUILDING PROGRESS:

 # SUBSCRIBERS: _____   **EMAILED THIS WEEK** ✉

SOCIAL MEDIA PROMO THIS WEEK:

☐ Twitter   ☐ Facebook   ☐ Pinterest   ☐ Instagram   ☐ YouTube   ☐ LinkedIn   ☐ Google+

EXTERNAL LINKS:

INTERNAL LINKS:

PRODUCTS PROMOTED:

☐ Affiliate Disclaimer Included

MARKETING PLANNER

TOP TRAFFIC CHANNELS:

MARKETING TO DO LIST:

FREE ADVERTISING IDEAS:

PAID ADVERTISING IDEAS:

MARKETING PLANNER

PROMOTIONAL STRATEGIES TO MAXIMIZE EXPOSURE

PROMOTIONAL IDEAS:

MARKETING TO DO:

SOCIAL MEDIA GROWTH TRACKER:

	BEFORE:	AFTER:
Facebook		
Instagram		
Twitter		
Pinterest		
YouTube		

OTHER:

LIST BUILDING & ENGAGEMENT:

- MAILING LIST SUBSCRIBERS:
- # OF EMAILS SENT TO SUBSCRIBERS:
- # OF NEW BLOG POSTS THIS WEEK:
- # OF COMPLETED GUEST POSTS:

NOTES:

GUEST BLOGGING

POST TITLE:

PUBLISH DATE: | CATEGORY:

MAIN TOPIC:

POST SUMMARY:

KEY POINTS:

INCLUDED LINKS: | SHARED ON: | FACEBOOK | INSTAGRAM
| | TWITTER | PINTEREST

TAGS & KEYWORDS: | # OF COMMENTS: | # OF TRACKBACKS:

NOTES:

SEPTEMBER

TASKS, MARKETING, ENGAGEMENT & MONETIZATION

CONTENT IDEAS

PROMOTION IDEAS

TOP PRIORITIES

MONTHLY FOCUS

MONETIZATION IDEAS

MONTHLY GOALS

MAIN OBJECTIVE:

GOAL:

ACTION STEPS:

GOAL:

ACTION STEPS:

GOAL:

ACTION STEPS:

TRAFFIC STATS:

MAILING LIST SUBSCRIBERS:

CONTENT PLANNER

POST TITLE:

PUBLICATION DATE:

TARGETED KEYWORDS:

TO DO CHECKLIST:

- Research Topic
- Pinpoint Target Audience
- Choose target keywords
- Optimize for search engines
- Link to other blog post
- Create post images
- Proofread & Edit Post
- Schedule Post Date

SOCIAL SHARING: (circle all that apply)

Facebook Twitter YouTube Pinterest LinkedIn Instagram

TOPIC OUTLINE:

NOTES:

CONTENT PLANNER

CATEGORY:

RESOURCE LINKS:

GRAPHICS/IMAGES:

KEY POINTS:

SEO CHECKLIST:

- Primary keyword in post title
- Secondary keyword in sub-title
- Keyword in first paragraph
- Word count > 1000 words
- 1-2 Outbound Links
- Internal Link Structure
- Post URL includes keywords
- Meta description added
- Post includes images
- Post includes sub-headlines
- Social sharing enabled

NOTES:

POST PLANNER

WEEK OF: _____

TYPE: ARTICLE: ☐   TUTORIAL: ☐   REVIEW: ☐   GUEST POST: ☐

PUBLICATION DATE:

TITLE:

CATEGORY:

KEYWORDS:

NOTES:

PUBLICATION DATE:

TITLE:

CATEGORY:

KEYWORDS:

NOTES:

PUBLICATION DATE:

TITLE:

CATEGORY:

KEYWORDS:

NOTES:

POST PLANNER

WEEK OF: _____

TYPE: ARTICLE: ☐   TUTORIAL: ☐   REVIEW: ☐   GUEST POST: ☐

PUBLICATION DATE:

TITLE:
CATEGORY:
KEYWORDS:
NOTES:

LIST BUILDING PROGRESS:

 # SUBSCRIBERS: _____   **EMAILED THIS WEEK** ✉

SOCIAL MEDIA PROMO THIS WEEK:

☐ Twitter   ☐ Facebook   ☐ Pinterest   ☐ Instagram   ☐ YouTube   ☐ LinkedIn   ☐ Google+

EXTERNAL LINKS:

PRODUCTS PROMOTED:

INTERNAL LINKS:

Affiliate Disclaimer Included

MARKETING PLANNER

TOP TRAFFIC CHANNELS:

MARKETING TO DO LIST:

FREE ADVERTISING IDEAS:

PAID ADVERTISING IDEAS:

MARKETING PLANNER

PROMOTIONAL STRATEGIES TO MAXIMIZE EXPOSURE

PROMOTIONAL IDEAS:

MARKETING TO DO:

SOCIAL MEDIA GROWTH TRACKER:

BEFORE: AFTER:

- Facebook
- Instagram
- Twitter
- Pinterest
- YouTube

OTHER:

LIST BUILDING & ENGAGEMENT:

MAILING LIST SUBSCRIBERS:

OF EMAILS SENT TO SUBSCRIBERS:

OF NEW BLOG POSTS THIS WEEK:

OF COMPLETED GUEST POSTS:

NOTES:

GUEST BLOGGING

POST TITLE:

| PUBLISH DATE: | CATEGORY: |

MAIN TOPIC:

POST SUMMARY:

KEY POINTS:

INCLUDED LINKS:

SHARED ON: FACEBOOK | INSTAGRAM | TWITTER | PINTEREST

TAGS & KEYWORDS:

 # OF COMMENTS: | **# OF TRACKBACKS:**

NOTES:

OCTOBER

TASKS, MARKETING, ENGAGEMENT & MONETIZATION

CONTENT IDEAS	PROMOTION IDEAS

TOP PRIORITIES

MONTHLY FOCUS	MONETIZATION IDEAS

MONTHLY GOALS

MAIN OBJECTIVE:

GOAL:

ACTION STEPS:

GOAL:

ACTION STEPS:

GOAL:

ACTION STEPS:

TRAFFIC STATS:

MAILING LIST SUBSCRIBERS:

CONTENT PLANNER

POST TITLE:

PUBLICATION DATE:

TARGETED KEYWORDS:

TO DO CHECKLIST:

- Research Topic
- Pinpoint Target Audience
- Choose target keywords
- Optimize for search engines
- Link to other blog post
- Create post images
- Proofread & Edit Post
- Schedule Post Date

SOCIAL SHARING: (circle all that apply)

Facebook Twitter YouTube Pinterest LinkedIn Instagram

TOPIC OUTLINE:

NOTES:

CONTENT PLANNER

CATEGORY:

RESOURCE LINKS:

GRAPHICS/IMAGES:

KEY POINTS:

SEO CHECKLIST:

- Primary keyword in post title
- Secondary keyword in sub-title
- Keyword in first paragraph
- Word count > 1000 words
- 1-2 Outbound Links
- Internal Link Structure
- Post URL includes keywords
- Meta description added
- Post includes images
- Post includes sub-headlines
- Social sharing enabled

NOTES:

POST PLANNER

WEEK OF: _____

TYPE: ARTICLE: ☐   TUTORIAL: ☐   REVIEW: ☐   GUEST POST: ☐

PUBLICATION DATE:

TITLE: _____

CATEGORY: _____

KEYWORDS: _____

NOTES: _____

PUBLICATION DATE:

TITLE: _____

CATEGORY: _____

KEYWORDS: _____

NOTES: _____

PUBLICATION DATE:

TITLE: _____

CATEGORY: _____

KEYWORDS: _____

NOTES: _____

POST PLANNER

WEEK OF: _____

TYPE: ARTICLE: ☐   TUTORIAL: ☐   REVIEW: ☐   GUEST POST: ☐

PUBLICATION DATE:

TITLE:

CATEGORY:

KEYWORDS:

NOTES:

LIST BUILDING PROGRESS:

 # SUBSCRIBERS: _____   **EMAILED THIS WEEK** ✉

SOCIAL MEDIA PROMO THIS WEEK:

☐ Twitter   ☐ Facebook   ☐ Pinterest   ☐ Instagram   ☐ YouTube   ☐ LinkedIn   ☐ Google+

EXTERNAL LINKS:

INTERNAL LINKS:

PRODUCTS PROMOTED:

Affiliate Disclaimer Included

MARKETING PLANNER

TOP TRAFFIC CHANNELS:

MARKETING TO DO LIST:

FREE ADVERTISING IDEAS:

PAID ADVERTISING IDEAS:

MARKETING PLANNER

PROMOTIONAL STRATEGIES TO MAXIMIZE EXPOSURE

PROMOTIONAL IDEAS:

MARKETING TO DO:

SOCIAL MEDIA GROWTH TRACKER:

	BEFORE:	AFTER:
Facebook		
Instagram		
Twitter		
Pinterest		
YouTube		

OTHER:

LIST BUILDING & ENGAGEMENT:

MAILING LIST SUBSCRIBERS:

 # OF EMAILS SENT TO SUBSCRIBERS:

 # OF NEW BLOG POSTS THIS WEEK:

 # OF COMPLETED GUEST POSTS:

NOTES:

GUEST BLOGGING

POST TITLE:

PUBLISH DATE: | CATEGORY:

MAIN TOPIC:

POST SUMMARY:

KEY POINTS:

INCLUDED LINKS: | **SHARED ON:** | FACEBOOK | INSTAGRAM
| | TWITTER | PINTEREST

TAGS & KEYWORDS:

OF COMMENTS: | # OF TRACKBACKS:

NOTES:

NOVEMBER

TASKS, MARKETING, ENGAGEMENT & MONETIZATION

CONTENT IDEAS

PROMOTION IDEAS

TOP PRIORITIES

MONTHLY FOCUS

MONETIZATION IDEAS

MONTHLY GOALS

MAIN OBJECTIVE:

GOAL:

ACTION STEPS:

GOAL:

ACTION STEPS:

GOAL:

ACTION STEPS:

TRAFFIC STATS:

MAILING LIST SUBSCRIBERS:

CONTENT PLANNER

POST TITLE:

PUBLICATION DATE:

TARGETED KEYWORDS:

TO DO CHECKLIST:

- Research Topic
- Pinpoint Target Audience
- Choose target keywords
- Optimize for search engines
- Link to other blog post
- Create post images
- Proofread & Edit Post
- Schedule Post Date

SOCIAL SHARING: (circle all that apply)

Facebook Twitter YouTube Pinterest LinkedIn Instagram

TOPIC OUTLINE:

NOTES:

CONTENT PLANNER

CATEGORY:

RESOURCE LINKS:

GRAPHICS/IMAGES:

KEY POINTS:

SEO CHECKLIST:

- Primary keyword in post title
- Secondary keyword in sub-title
- Keyword in first paragraph
- Word count > 1000 words
- 1-2 Outbound Links
- Internal Link Structure
- Post URL includes keywords
- Meta description added
- Post includes images
- Post includes sub-headlines
- Social sharing enabled

NOTES:

POST PLANNER

WEEK OF: _____

TYPE: ARTICLE: ☐   TUTORIAL: ☐   REVIEW: ☐   GUEST POST: ☐

PUBLICATION DATE:

TITLE:

CATEGORY:

KEYWORDS:

NOTES:

PUBLICATION DATE:

TITLE:

CATEGORY:

KEYWORDS:

NOTES:

PUBLICATION DATE:

TITLE:

CATEGORY:

KEYWORDS:

NOTES:

POST PLANNER

WEEK OF: _____

TYPE: ARTICLE: ☐   TUTORIAL: ☐   REVIEW: ☐   GUEST POST: ☐

PUBLICATION DATE:

TITLE:

CATEGORY:

KEYWORDS:

NOTES:

LIST BUILDING PROGRESS:

 # SUBSCRIBERS: _____   **EMAILED THIS WEEK** ✉

SOCIAL MEDIA PROMO THIS WEEK:

☐ Twitter ☐ Facebook ☐ Pinterest ☐ Instagram ☐ YouTube ☐ LinkedIn ☐ Google+

EXTERNAL LINKS:

PRODUCTS PROMOTED:

INTERNAL LINKS:

☐ Affiliate Disclaimer Included

POST PLANNER

WEEK OF: _____

TYPE: ARTICLE: ☐   TUTORIAL: ☐   REVIEW: ☐   GUEST POST: ☐

PUBLICATION DATE:

TITLE:

CATEGORY:

KEYWORDS:

NOTES:

LIST BUILDING PROGRESS:

 # SUBSCRIBERS: _____   **EMAILED THIS WEEK** ✉

SOCIAL MEDIA PROMO THIS WEEK:

☐ Twitter   ☐ Facebook   ☐ Pinterest   ☐ Instagram   ☐ YouTube   ☐ LinkedIn   ☐ Google+

EXTERNAL LINKS:

INTERNAL LINKS:

PRODUCTS PROMOTED:

Affiliate Disclaimer Included

MARKETING PLANNER

TOP TRAFFIC CHANNELS:

MARKETING TO DO LIST:

FREE ADVERTISING IDEAS:

PAID ADVERTISING IDEAS:

MARKETING PLANNER

PROMOTIONAL STRATEGIES TO MAXIMIZE EXPOSURE

PROMOTIONAL IDEAS:

MARKETING TO DO:

SOCIAL MEDIA GROWTH TRACKER:

BEFORE: AFTER:

f
[Instagram]
[Twitter]
[Pinterest]
[YouTube]

OTHER:

LIST BUILDING & ENGAGEMENT:

MAILING LIST SUBSCRIBERS:

 # OF EMAILS SENT TO SUBSCRIBERS:

 # OF NEW BLOG POSTS THIS WEEK:

 # OF COMPLETED GUEST POSTS:

NOTES:

GUEST BLOGGING

POST TITLE:

PUBLISH DATE: | CATEGORY:

MAIN TOPIC:

POST SUMMARY:

KEY POINTS:

INCLUDED LINKS: | SHARED ON: | FACEBOOK | INSTAGRAM
| | TWITTER | PINTEREST

TAGS & KEYWORDS: | # OF COMMENTS: | # OF TRACKBACKS:

NOTES:

DECEMBER

TASKS, MARKETING, ENGAGEMENT & MONETIZATION

CONTENT IDEAS

PROMOTION IDEAS

TOP PRIORITIES

MONTHLY FOCUS

MONETIZATION IDEAS

MONTHLY GOALS

MAIN OBJECTIVE:

GOAL:

ACTION STEPS:

GOAL:

ACTION STEPS:

GOAL:

ACTION STEPS:

TRAFFIC STATS:

MAILING LIST SUBSCRIBERS:

CONTENT PLANNER

POST TITLE:

PUBLICATION DATE:

TARGETED KEYWORDS:

TO DO CHECKLIST:

- Research Topic
- Pinpoint Target Audience
- Choose target keywords
- Optimize for search engines
- Link to other blog post
- Create post images
- Proofread & Edit Post
- Schedule Post Date

SOCIAL SHARING: (circle all that apply)

TOPIC OUTLINE:

NOTES:

CONTENT PLANNER

CATEGORY:

RESOURCE LINKS:

GRAPHICS/IMAGES:

KEY POINTS:

SEO CHECKLIST:

- Primary keyword in post title
- Secondary keyword in sub-title
- Keyword in first paragraph
- Word count > 1000 words
- 1-2 Outbound Links
- Internal Link Structure
- Post URL includes keywords
- Meta description added
- Post includes images
- Post includes sub-headlines
- Social sharing enabled

NOTES:

POST PLANNER

WEEK OF: _____

TYPE: ARTICLE: ☐   TUTORIAL: ☐   REVIEW: ☐   GUEST POST: ☐

PUBLICATION DATE:

TITLE:

CATEGORY:

KEYWORDS:

NOTES:

PUBLICATION DATE:

TITLE:

CATEGORY:

KEYWORDS:

NOTES:

PUBLICATION DATE:

TITLE:

CATEGORY:

KEYWORDS:

NOTES:

POST PLANNER

WEEK OF: _____

TYPE: ARTICLE: ☐   TUTORIAL: ☐   REVIEW: ☐   GUEST POST: ☐

PUBLICATION DATE:

TITLE: _____

CATEGORY: _____

KEYWORDS: _____

NOTES: _____

LIST BUILDING PROGRESS:

 # SUBSCRIBERS: _____   **EMAILED THIS WEEK** ✉

SOCIAL MEDIA PROMO THIS WEEK:

☐ Twitter   ☐ Facebook   ☐ Pinterest   ☐ Instagram   ☐ YouTube   ☐ LinkedIn   ☐ Google+

EXTERNAL LINKS:

PRODUCTS PROMOTED:

INTERNAL LINKS:

Affiliate Disclaimer Included

MARKETING PLANNER

TOP TRAFFIC CHANNELS:

MARKETING TO DO LIST:

FREE ADVERTISING IDEAS:

PAID ADVERTISING IDEAS:

MARKETING PLANNER

PROMOTIONAL STRATEGIES TO MAXIMIZE EXPOSURE

PROMOTIONAL IDEAS:

MARKETING TO DO:

SOCIAL MEDIA GROWTH TRACKER:

BEFORE: AFTER:

- Facebook
- Instagram
- Twitter
- Pinterest
- YouTube

OTHER:

LIST BUILDING & ENGAGEMENT:

MAILING LIST SUBSCRIBERS:

 # OF EMAILS SENT TO SUBSCRIBERS:

 # OF NEW BLOG POSTS THIS WEEK:

 # OF COMPLETED GUEST POSTS:

NOTES:

GUEST BLOGGING

POST TITLE:

PUBLISH DATE:	CATEGORY:

MAIN TOPIC:

POST SUMMARY:

KEY POINTS:

INCLUDED LINKS:

SHARED ON:

FACEBOOK	INSTAGRAM
TWITTER	PINTEREST

TAGS & KEYWORDS:

 # OF COMMENTS: **# OF TRACKBACKS:**

NOTES:

CPSIA information can be obtained
at www.ICGtesting.com
Printed in the USA
LVHW100234071220
673517LV00013B/773

9 781075 301322